A GUY'S GUIDE

Body Double

Understanding Physical Changes

ABDO
Publishing Company

A GUY'S GUIDE

Body Double

Understanding Physical Changes

by Tad Kershner

Content Consultant
Dr. Robyn J. A. Silverman
Child/Teen Development Expert and Success Coach
Powerful Words Character Development

Credits

Published by ABDO Publishing Company, 8000 West 78th Street, Edina, Minnesota 55439. Copyright © 2011 by Abdo Consulting Group, Inc. International copyrights reserved in all countries. No part of this book may be reproduced in any form without written permission from the publisher. The Essential Library™ is a trademark and logo of ABDO Publishing Company.

Printed in the United States of America,
North Mankato, Minnesota
062010
092010

♻ THIS BOOK CONTAINS AT LEAST 10% RECYCLED MATERIALS.

Editor: Rebecca Rowell
Copy Editor: Nick Cafarelli
Interior Design and Production: Marie Tupy
Cover Design: Craig Hinton

Library of Congress Cataloging-in-Publication Data
Kershner, Tad, 1967–
    Body double : understanding physical changes / Tad Kershner.
       p. cm. — (Essential health : a guy's guide)
    Includes index.
    ISBN 978-1-61613-538-6
    1. Puberty—Juvenile literature. 2. Teenage boys—Physiology—Juvenile literature. I. Title.
    RJ143.K47 2010
    613.9'53—dc22
                                        2010017077

contents

Dr. Robyn Silverman truly enjoys spending time with young people. In fact, it's what she does best! As a child and teen development specialist, Dr. Robyn has devoted her career to helping guys just like you become all they can be—and possibly more than they ever imagined. Throughout this series, you'll read her expert advice on friends, girls, classmates, school, family, and everything in between.

A self-esteem and body image expert, Dr. Robyn takes a positive approach to life. She knows how tough it is to be a kid in today's world, and she's prepared with encouragement and guidance to help you become your very best and realize your goals.

Dr. Robyn helps young people share their wildest dreams and biggest problems. Her compassion, openness, and honesty make her trusted by many adolescents, and she considers it a gift to be able to interact with the young people whom she sees as the leaders of tomorrow. She created the Powerful Words Character Development system, a program taught all over the world in martial arts and other sports programs to help guys just like you become examples to others in their communities.

As a speaker, success coach, and award-winning author, Dr. Robyn's powerful messages have reached thousands of people. Her expert advice has been featured in *Prevention* magazine, *Parenting* magazine, *U.S. News and World Report*, and the *Washington Post*. She was an expert for *The Tyra Show, Fox News,* and NBC's *LXtv.* She has an online presence, too. You can follow her on Twitter, become a fan on Facebook, and read her blog on her Web site, www.DrRobynSilverman.com. When she isn't working, Dr. Robyn enjoys spending time with her family in New Jersey.

Dr. Robyn believes that young people are assets to be developed, not problems to be fixed. As she puts it, "Guys are so much more than the way the media paints them. They have so many things to offer. I'm ready to highlight how guys get it right and tips for the ways they can make their teen years the best years so far . . . I'd be grateful if you'd come along for the ride."

Adolescence is a time of change. You may feel suddenly like everything's different—your body, your thoughts, your emotions, and perhaps even your relationships with others. You used to be pretty sure of what you were feeling and why. Now, you may feel mad, sad, or scared all at once. And it may seem as though there's no logical reason for any of it.

You might be struggling with where you are right now, stuck in the middle of a storm of change—or waiting anxiously to start changing. Parents, doctors, books, and health class will all tell a guy that the changes he's experiencing, or is about to experience, are perfectly natural. Still, he may feel anxious and unhappy because he suddenly looks a lot different than he used to or wants to.

In my early teen years, my body always felt clumsy. I was continually dropping or banging into things. I thought it was part of who I was as a person and that I would be like that forever. I couldn't imagine how I'd ever be able to function in the adult world. Then one day, I was taking my books out of my locker when I realized that I couldn't remember the last time I had dropped them or bumped into anything. I had grown out of my clumsiness so naturally that I hadn't even noticed.

During that time, the whole world seemed to revolve around popularity. Looking around me, I saw that both the unpopular guys and the popular guys were all going through the same physical changes. The only difference seemed to be how the guys in the two groups reacted. Usually, the popular ones made a joke out of it. Often, the unpopular ones acted as though they were somehow defective— this sometimes led to people treating them that way.

I hope the stories in this book will be helpful as you go through your own changes. The process may not be easy, but it doesn't have to be overwhelming. And it's actually quite amazing, though you may not feel that way. You will look and sound different than you did before, but you are still you, and there's no better person to be than who you are.

Good luck,
Tad

1

The Gentle Giant

o two bodies are alike. And these days, your body may differ from one day to the next. When struggling with the changes of adolescence, it may be tempting to believe that everyone else has it easier than you. For example, smaller guys may be envious of larger guys. To the smaller guys, it seems like those bigger than them could simply overpower anybody who gives them a hard time.

But larger guys have their own struggles. They are targets for bullies because beating the big kid is the best way for a bully to gain an instant reputation. And that's exactly what Jonathan discovered.

Jonathan's Story

Even though he was in seventh grade, most people thought Jonathan was in high school. He had always been tall as a kid. Then, he hit puberty well before other guys in school. During the summer, he had an incredible growth spurt and now towered over his classmates. Many kids called him "Giant John."

A lot of guys enjoyed picking fights with Jonathan. He didn't want to fight anyone and did his best to ignore those who teased and taunted him. The one time he stood up for himself, he got into trouble. Everyone blamed Jonathan

Larger guys are targets for bullies because beating the big kid is the best way for a bully to gain an instant reputation.

because he was so big. They assumed he had to have started the fight.

David especially liked to torment Jonathan. David and his friends always gathered around him and yelled, "Hey Stretch! What's the weather like up there?" They stuck out their legs and tried to trip him. Jonathan loved school, but being picked on was getting to him. He wished everyone would just leave him alone.

Think About It

- Have you ever felt like another guy must have it a lot better or easier than you? What do you think was really the case for that person? What challenges might he have been facing?

- Why does David like to tease Jonathan so much? What could he gain from picking on Jonathan?

- What opinions do you think people have formed about you based on your appearance?

One day after English class, Jonathan saw David and his two friends surround Craig Snow, one of the smallest guys in school.

"Shrimp! . . . Wimp!" they taunted him. David and his crew shoved Craig into his locker.

Jonathan walked far around the group to avoid being noticed. When he looked back at the scene, he realized how small David really was. The bully was not much bigger than Craig. Jonathan clenched his hands into fists—he was so mad! He knew he could easily push them out of the way, but he didn't want to get in trouble. If he got sent to Principal Rosso's office, what are the chances she'd see things his way?

David and his buddies taunted Jonathan for being too big, and they picked on Craig for being too small. What did they want?

All through his history class, Jonathan replayed the incident in his mind. He kept seeing David slam Craig into his locker. David and his buddies taunted Jonathan for being too big, and they picked on Craig for being too small. What did they want?

A few days later, Jonathan saw David messing with Vince during gym. That afternoon, Jonathan was in the bathroom when David snuck up behind Will and gave him a wedgie. Neither Vince nor Will even stood up for themselves.

Jonathan thought it was stupid that everyone was so afraid of David. Jonathan decided he had had enough. It was time to do something about David.

That night, Jonathan's mind was racing too fast for sleeping. He kept thinking through plans for stopping David. In the morning, he knew what he would do. He didn't have to face David alone—neither did anyone else.

Think About It

- Do you think Jonathan is right that the principal wouldn't understand if he stopped the bullies from picking on Craig? Why or why not?

- What would you have done in Jonathan's situation? Would you have tried to help the smaller guy?

- What are some of the options Jonathan has for stopping David from being a bully?

The next day, Jonathan approached Craig in the hall after the last class let out to share his idea

for stopping David. Craig took one look at Jonathan
walking toward him and started backing away,
leaving the door to his locker wide open.

"Hey," Jonathan called out to Craig, "Wait!
I just want to talk to you! I'm not going to hurt you.
I want to help."

Craig slowly walked back to his locker. Craig smiled as Jonathan outlined his plan. Together, the two of them went to find Vince. They found him outside waiting to be picked up. Like Craig, Vince smiled as he listened to Jonathan's plan.

Jonathan discovered that the other guys were pretty cool. Craig was wickedly funny and could do the best Yoda voice. He kept saying, "Use the force." And Vince had an awesome collection of radio-controlled model airplanes. By the next afternoon, other students joined the original three to become one of the biggest groups in the school.

By the end of the week, the newfound friends had a chance to follow through with their plan. After school, David cornered Craig at his locker. But things didn't go as usual for the bully. He suddenly found himself surrounded by ten guys. David swallowed and backed up a step. "Look, it's King Shrimp and the Planktons," he said.

Jonathan didn't hesitate to respond, "Yep. We're getting T-shirts made." He and his friends stood their ground. Initially, the bully froze. He seemed uncertain about what to do. Finally, David slunk away. The guys smiled as they watched David head down the hall and out the door—alone.

think about it

- what are some of the advantages to being really big or really small?

- Have you ever done something for one reason and then discovered it had a benefit you hadn't anticipated?

- what, if anything, would you have you done differently to deal with David?

Many experts liken bullies to wolves—they roam the school seeking easy prey. The bully will pick on a guy who stands out from the others for *any* reason. Once the bully finds such an individual, he will try to dominate his target in an attempt to get his victim to submit. Although the attacks may feel very personal, they rarely are. The bully is simply looking to put himself in control by finding others he can overpower.

Although strong words may be used, most of a bully's power plays are achieved through body language. Stand up for yourself using your own powerful body language: Stand straight and tall, speak clearly, and make eye contact. Submissive body language includes hunching, shrinking, lack of eye contact, and speaking quietly. Standing this way, you can send the message that you're an easy target.

A guy who backs down from a bully is showing submission, and he will most likely continue to be bullied. A guy who fights a bully may provoke him even more, but a guy who dismisses a bully with a simple "whatever" attitude is most likely to be left alone in the future. Dismissive guys are too much work for too little reward, so the bully will most likely seek easier targets elsewhere.

Work It Out

1. Bullies tend to pick on guys less when those guys have several reliable friends. Banding with other guys can be a good way to achieve both protection and friendship.

2. It can be challenging to ignore bullies. Find a friend or an adult you trust and role-play different scenarios together. Practice using assertive words and body language that is not submissive. With practice, it can become much easier to use these strategies when confronted by the real thing.

The Last Word from Tad

Remember, there's no right size when it comes to people. And, while you can't control when your body grows or how tall you will become, you can learn to accept and appreciate your body no matter what. You can also control how you respond to others who might pick on you for your size. Those two things—accepting your body and being dismissive of bullies—will go a long way toward helping you cope when problems come up.

2

The Too-Big Body

s guys mature, they develop a sense of their own identity. While well-meaning adults tell guys that what is inside is most important, it may often seem that looks matter more. This seems especially so when judgments people form are usually based on appearance.

More than any time in history, our culture is influenced by a constant flood of media images. Television, movies, magazines, and the Internet all contribute to a belief that the only way to be attractive and popular is to be strong and handsome.

It can be easy for a guy to let himself be defined by other people's

beliefs without really questioning those beliefs and their validity. Dylan lived his life in shame for a long time because he didn't fit any current definitions of attractiveness. One day, he got sick of it and decided to make a change.

Dylan's Story

Dylan always liked when Kaitlin stood up in English class to read, because it meant he could watch her without feeling embarrassed. He loved her long hair that she always held back with a gold clip, and he was mesmerized by her green eyes.

Television, movies, magazines, and the Internet all contribute to a belief that the only way to be attractive and popular is to be strong and handsome.

One day, Dylan was admiring Kaitlin when Ashley waved her hand in front of his eyes. "What you staring at, Lard Ass?" she sneered.

"Blimpy thinks he has a chance with her," Rena said, and then laughed.

"Fatty'd roll over on top of her and squish her like a pancake," said Wyatt. He laughed and made squishing sounds.

As the other kids snickered, Dylan could feel his eyes burning. He shrunk down in his desk, wishing he was dead.

The bell finally rang. Dylan snuck away to an isolated corner of the school. He looked around to make sure no one was watching before taking a candy bar from his backpack. He wondered why everyone was so mean to him.

Whenever he thought about how everyone laughed at him, Dylan wanted to eat—it seemed to take away his pain. But then he felt bad about eating. He'd never get strong or athletic that way. When he got hurt in gym, aspirin stopped the physical pain. He wished there was something to end the pain he felt inside. He slid the uneaten candy bar back into his bag.

Think About It

- Have you ever had a crush on someone who seemed unreachable? What was it like? What did you do?

- Have you ever had something so embarrassing happen that you wished you could disappear? How did you deal with it?

- Why does Dylan take out a candy bar? Why does he go to an isolated area of the school to do it?

- What do you do to feel better when you're feeling sad or stressed?

Dylan always heard the words together: fat and lazy. But he always worked really hard on diets. While the other kids were out doing something fun, he was usually forcing himself through another three pounds of celery or scouring the Internet for a new diet that might finally be the magical cure to make him lose weight.

When he got home from school that day, Dylan was still stinging over the Kaitlin incident. While he tried to concentrate on his math homework, Dylan had a chocolate bar open and halfway to his mouth before he stopped himself. It had become such a habit for him to eat, but he was working on changing that behavior.

To distract himself, Dylan started looking around the house for things to juggle. He picked up three rolls of toilet paper. As he tossed them around, the paper unspooled, covering him like a mummy.

His little brother, Jeremy, giggled with laughter. "That's so funny! You gotta put that on YouTube."

"Nobody wants to watch a fat kid throw stuff in the air," Dylan responded.

Think About It

- why does everyone assume that Dylan is lazy because of his size?
- what talents do you have that no one knows about?
- what stops you from showing off those talents to others?

Dylan found himself thinking about a juggling video all the next day. He wrote little bits of script

for himself in different classes. He was glad to focus on that in English class because he didn't dare look at Kaitlin after what had happened the day before.

When Dylan got home, he had Jeremy record him. He launched into his best "mockumentary" announcer voice while juggling all kinds of outrageous things. Dylan ended every segment by saying, "Hey Batman, juggle this!"

Jeremy laughed so hard they had to start over three times because he kept shaking the video camera. Finally, the brothers got enough footage for a good short film. Dylan edited it together and put it online, posting the link on his Web site.

For the first time in weeks, he felt that he was being seen for something more than just his size.

For the next few days, he kept waiting for someone at school to see it—maybe even Kaitlin.

But nothing happened. The days dragged by as they always did, and the same kids kept teasing him.

Dylan decided it had been a dumb idea. His video was lost out there with zillions of others no one would ever see.

But then the next Monday, Wyatt called out to Dylan in the hall. "Hey Batman, juggle this!" he said, tossing Dylan an apple and a CD. Dylan caught the stuff. Then he grabbed his phone and his iPod to add to the mix.

As the objects flew over his head, Dylan grinned. For the first time in weeks, he felt that he was being seen for something more than just his size.

Think About It

- How do you think others might feel about you if they knew about your hidden talents?

- What talents do you think people at school might have that they aren't sharing?

- If there's someone you find interesting at school, how might you reach out to him or her? What could you talk about with that person?

The variety of diet books, infomercials, Web sites, television programs, weight-loss products, and diet gurus is clear evidence that U.S. society is fixated on weight and size. But there isn't one right size for everyone. Some people are naturally larger than others. Others have medical reasons why they are overweight. Some eat for comfort because they are stressed or simply because they find it reassuring. It can be difficult for a person to change long-standing habits. Just because a guy is considered medically overweight does not mean he is lazy.

If you do want to lose weight, it is especially important to discuss any diets or nutrition products with a doctor. Many diets have been found to be harmful, and almost all of them can cause ill effects if they are not followed properly. Quick weight loss, fad diets, and overexercising are not healthy. Safe diets are not really "diets" at all—but rather, healthy, balanced ways of eating, exercising, and resting that result in maintaining a healthy weight and a healthy way of life.

Work It Out

If you feel you are turning to food for unhealthy reasons, make a list of four or five things you can do instead of eating when you feel stressed. They should be things you can do almost anywhere, such as drawing or chewing sugar-free gum.

Studies often show that diets don't work. Ask your doctor about healthy options before changing the way you eat.

Talk to an adult you trust about your feelings about your weight. Many people have the same challenges as you, and it often helps to discover you are not alone in facing them.

It's important for everyone to eat healthy foods. Carry healthy foods with you at all times, such as carrots, nuts, or apples, which are good to snack on.

Exercise!

The Last Word from Tad

By putting himself out there with his juggling movie, Dylan made it easy for the other kids to talk to him. Humor is one of the best ways to open yourself to others. It also relieves some of the tension you may be feeling. It may take a lot of courage to be the center of attention and share your humor, but the results can be more than worth the risk.

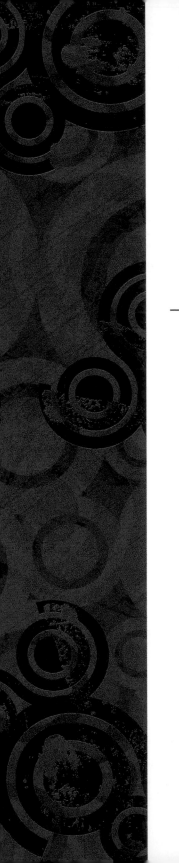

3

The Uncontrollable Voice

ll the changes that guys go through during adolescence seem designed to create maximum embarrassment. A face that won't stop breaking out and an awkward new body are bad enough. But living with a cracking, squeaky voice may seem like the ultimate dirty trick biology can play when a guy can't open his mouth without sounding like he belongs on a bad sitcom.

A guy who is used to being popular can suddenly find himself the subject of cruel teasing when his voice begins to change. And hearing adults say that these changes are all temporary doesn't really help much. Sometimes, unexpected

situations can throw a guy's entire life into chaos. He may not be able to change such an awkward dilemma, but he can always control how he responds to it. That's exactly what Jin learned.

Jin's Story

Jin loved drawing more than anything. He drew giant space battles and cartoons about funny things that happened at school. Girls loved when he drew pictures for them of horses or vampires or celebrities in manga style. The girls hung up his drawings in their lockers. The margins of Jin's school notebooks were filled with sketches.

Living with a cracking, squeaky voice may seem like the ultimate dirty trick biology can play when a guy can't open his mouth without sounding like he belongs on a bad sitcom.

His parents said it was fine as long as he studied hard and kept up his grades, which he did.

One Friday, all of his studying was about to pay off. He was on his way to ace his oral report in geography when his phone buzzed. He flipped open the screen and saw a text from Emily: "ru goin 2 beths bday 2moro?"

Emily wanted Jin at the party! Jin imagined his immediate future. Today: Ace report! Tomorrow: Spend an entire afternoon with Emily! Sunday: Fly to California to stay with Cousin Hao—no school for a whole week!

Jin made a final run-through of his report in his mind as he headed to class. Finally, it was his turn. He smiled at Emily and stood up confidently, not even looking at his note cards. "PatAAgOnia hAs the wOrld's," he started to say. What was happening?! He sounded like a mouse being tortured. Little bursts of laughter broke the silence in the room. He knew all about voice changes from health class, but he never imagined he could sound this awful.

Jin tried again. This time, his voice squawked like a rusty garage door spring, and everyone seemed to laugh, including his best friend, Zach. Jin didn't dare look at Emily.

THINK ABOUT IT

- Have you ever had a day suddenly take an unexpected turn for the worse? How did you react?
- Why did it hurt Jin when Zach laughed?
- When have you done something embarrassing and then forced yourself to keep going even after feeling so self-conscious?

The following afternoon, Jin was lying on his back in his room staring at the ceiling with his iPod cranked. It was 2:30, and everyone would be at Beth's party by then. Maybe Emily was wearing that black dress she had worn for picture day. He tested his voice. It squeaked on Emily's name.

At 3:15, Jin's phone buzzed with a text from Beth: "Where RU? :("

Jin decided it was too late to go to the party. Besides, everyone there would just laugh at him again. He couldn't take the embarrassment.

Later that afternoon, Jin's mom brought him some soup and chocolate chip cookies. "You should have gone to the party, honey. No one cares what you sound like," she said.

He sat up and asked, "Why did this have to happen right now?"

"Every boy goes through this, Jin," his mom said. "You don't get to decide when it happens, unfortunately. Your body is doing what it is supposed to do. I know it's hard, especially when you have no control over the situation. It may seem as though it will last forever, but it will go away. Besides, any friend who makes fun of you isn't really your friend anyway." She tousled his hair.

Jin pulled away. "Mom, don't do that! Just leave me alone!"

After she left, Jin buried his head under his pillow. He knew from health and biology classes that his mom was right, but it didn't change the fact that he was embarrassed. At least he still had the California trip to look forward to. Maybe his voice would be better by the time he got back.

Think About It

- Have you ever had to make a decision when you didn't like any of the options? What happened?

- Was there ever a time when you felt like your parents didn't understand you or something you were going through?

- How could Jin have handled Beth's party differently?

Jin did his best to avoid speaking during the flight. When he arrived in California, Jin was in for a surprise. Hao met him at baggage claim with a loud, "HeEY JiIn." Jin couldn't believe what he heard.

Hao was wearing his baseball uniform. "Hope you don't mind if we hit the game first," he rasped. "I'm pitching."

Though he liked baseball and wanted to support his cousin, Jin's heart sank. He hated meeting crowds of new people, and it would be even worse with his voice like this. But he didn't want to let down his cousin. "SuUre. NoO prOblem," he said. "It'll be fun!"

Jin sat in the stands with Hao's parents, dreading when it would be over and he'd have to

meet Hao's friends. Jin didn't feel much like cheering, even when his cousin hit a home run.

    After the game, Hao jogged over with two really cute girls. "HeEy cUHz!" Hao croaked. Jin cringed, but his cousin just exaggerated the screech even more and played it for comedy. "ThIIs is JeHessicAh and AHmandAAAAH!" The girls giggled, and Jessica ran her hand through Hao's hair.

Jin took a deep breath and stuck out his hand. "GlAAd to mEEyt you." He imitated Hao's absurd squeaks. The girls laughed.

Jin spent the afternoon with his cousin and new friends. When Hao's voice cracked, he laughed at himself, and the girls laughed, too. Jin made fun of his own crazy voice and found he really didn't care anymore that it was out of control. He even made it crack on purpose, just to hear the girls giggle. That afternoon was the most fun Jin had had in a long time. He couldn't wait to get home and try out his new moves with his own friends and schoolmates.

Think About It

- Have you ever tried acting like someone else for a while? What did you learn from the experience?

- What is the difference between copying someone and learning from them?

- How can you learn from someone and still be yourself?

- Have you ever made something you were embarrassed about into a joke?

A scratchy, squeaky voice is an embarrassing change of adolescence that goes away by itself. A guy's voice changes when his vocal cords begin to grow in size and mass. During this time, his entire larynx is also growing. This means that the tonal characteristics of his voice are continually changing. Some guys may experience dramatic unsteadiness for a long time, while others have a rapid change or one that may be hardly noticeable at all.

When a guy's voice changes, he may want to hide from everyone so that he avoids any chance of feeling embarrassed. But this is not the answer. Every guy's voice changes. Your friends will want to be around you because of who you are, not because of how you sound.

Work It Out

1. Take care of your throat. When it feels sore, a hot beverage such as tea with lemon can be soothing, as can herbal cough drops. Stay away from throat treatments for colds and flu, as they contain unnecessary medication. Avoid talking loudly in noisy places, don't smoke, and keep away from secondhand smoke.

2. Your changing voice may be disruptive, especially if you act or sing. Your body works on its own time, so don't be surprised if a voice change coincides with something important, such as an audition or a performance. At the first sign of a voice change, let your theater or choir director know what's going on. He or she can plan with you to be prepared.

3. Don't worry! However awful your voice may sound, the chances are very good that everything is going according to plan, and your voice change will work itself out in time. If your throat feels bad for an extended period, check with your parent, guardian, or doctor.

The Last Word from Tad

When I was growing up, my family went to a church that started the service with singing. One of my favorite songs had a chorus where the men came in with a glorious deep bass line. As a young teen, I kept trying to sing that bass part when I was alone. I was always too high or too scratchy. One day, I finally hit a low note I hadn't been able to sing. I could feel it rumbling in my throat as I'd never felt before. That Sunday, I couldn't wait for the chorus. When the time came, I stood up with the other men, and I sounded good. That has always been a proud moment in my life.

4

Send Muscles Now!

Every guy develops muscles at a different rate. Some guys seem to fill out automatically with no effort whatsoever. Some grow muscles as a result of sports or other activities. And some have to work really hard at it.

It can feel discouraging to see other guys with more athletic bodies. Fortunately, this is one area where a guy has some control. Just as studying improves the brain and practicing an instrument improves skill with it, exercising the body builds strength and muscle definition.

Like anything else, exercise can be taken too far. Working out should be balanced with the other important

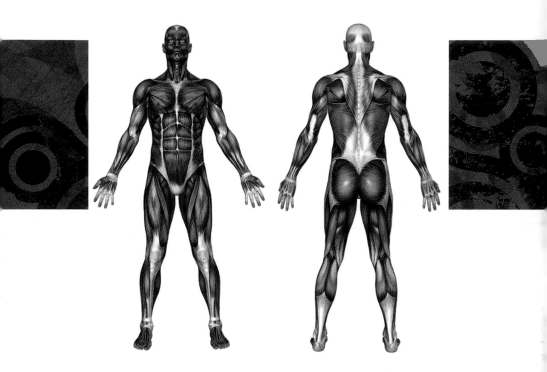

activities in a guy's life. When done right, weight training can help a guy feel good about himself. A guy doesn't have to be a jock to want to look better or be stronger. Any guy who wants a slightly different body can take action to do something about it, just as Deon did.

Deon's Story

Deon felt like a scarecrow. All the guys were developing muscles, but Deon's arms looked like sticks, and his legs

Just as studying improves the brain and practicing an instrument improves skill with it, exercising the body builds strength and muscle definition.

weren't much better. His mom kept saying he was "a slow developer," but it seemed that his body just wasn't interested in growing muscles. Deon wished he could go back to fifth grade when it hadn't mattered. Now, the girls all liked the muscular guys, and he knew he had no chance for a girl to even look at him.

One night, Deon's dad found him staring moodily at the bathroom mirror. He put his big arm around Deon's shoulders. "When I was your age, it seemed like all my friends had muscles, and I was going to look wimpy forever. One day, I decided I was sick and tired of it, so I went down to the Y and gave it a shot. After a couple months, I built some pretty good muscles."

Deon looked at his big, strong dad. He might have been smaller once, but he couldn't have ever been as small as Deon. "You should check out your weight room at school. I could help you make a plan," said Deon's dad.

"Sure, Dad," Deon replied, even though he knew he was no jock.

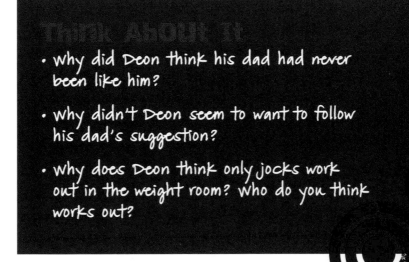

Think About It

- why did Deon think his dad had never been like him?

- why didn't Deon seem to want to follow his dad's suggestion?

- why does Deon think only jocks work out in the weight room? who do you think works out?

A week later, sign-up sheets were posted for athletic activities for the upcoming quarter: basketball, swimming, or weight training. If Deon picked weights, he could skip basketball, but he was certain everyone would make fun of him in the weight room just as they did on the basketball court. During lunch, he went to the weight room. The weight lifting assistant coach was sitting in a corner of the room, busy filling out papers. Even without guys working out, the room still reeked of smelly gym socks. Deon put the pin on the lowest weight and laid down on the bench.

He took a deep breath and pushed hard. The bar shot up, and the weight clanged at the top. *Wow!* he thought. *That was amazingly easy.* He moved the pin down two slots and still pushed it easily. He finished ten reps and moved on to the other machines. By the time he was done, he had only a few minutes left to take a quick shower.

Deon's whole body ached, but he felt good all over. The last few reps had been tough, but he was proud of himself for finishing. He'd been surprised to discover that his body wasn't as wimpy as it looked.

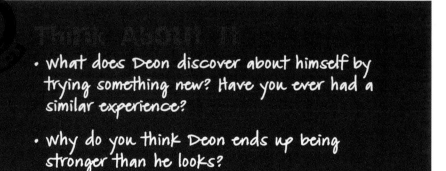

Think About It

- what does Deon discover about himself by trying something new? Have you ever had a similar experience?

- why do you think Deon ends up being stronger than he looks?

The next day, Deon ate his lunch on morning break so he could sneak into the weight room again. This time, he tired quickly. Maybe going every day wouldn't work. That night, he searched online for "weight training" and discovered that it really was better to alternate days and let his muscles rest while they grew. After an hour on his computer, he had a plan. He couldn't wait to try it the following week.

When sign-up time came, Deon saw all the names of the jocks on the list for weight training. He wasn't ready to work out in front of them, so he signed up for swimming and kept going to the weight room during lunch and after school. It was fun to have a secret project. He started noticing changes. His arms weren't so sticklike anymore. With more work, he might look pretty decent. And he loved the feeling of working out.

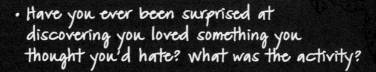

- Have you ever been surprised at discovering you loved something you thought you'd hate? What was the activity?

- How do you think Deon's growing body affects the way he feels about himself?

It can seem unfair that some guys get muscles without any effort while other guys have to work really hard at getting them. The good thing is that you do have a choice, and you really can do something about your muscles. Changing your body in a healthy way can make you feel great. Just be sure that whatever you're doing is to make your body the way you want it, not to fit someone else's idea of what you should look like.

In weight training, each exercise is designed to work specific muscle groups. The three things you can vary are weight, repetitions (reps), and sets (the number of times you run through the routine). You will get better and better with practice. Practicing with weight builds strength, while practicing repetitions builds endurance. For a good balance that builds both strength and endurance, try ten repetitions at 75 percent of your maximum capacity. Rest is also important. Try a full body workout Monday, Wednesday, and Friday and something else on Tuesday and Thursday or work the upper body on Monday, Wednesday, and Friday and the lower body on Tuesday and Thursday. Stay at the same weight for a week or two, and then raise it to the next notch.

1. Have a plan for working out. Your coach or doctor can help you, or there are a number of good books by reputable experts.

2. When using exercise machines or free weights, be sure to have adult supervision to prevent injury.

3. Don't go too fast. When starting something new, it's easy to take on too much and end up hating it or hurting yourself.

4. Charting your progress is a great motivator. It's satisfying to see your numbers increase as you grow stronger.

5. If weights aren't your thing, try any activity that works the muscles you want to improve. Watching how decisions you make shape your body can be powerful.

6. Don't worry about what other people can or can't do—this is about you being healthy.

The Last Word from Tad

It can be challenging to step into a room of people who are fit and have defined muscles when you don't feel that way at all. Try not to focus on others. Think about your goal to be healthier and stronger. Dedication will pay off with a healthy change in your body and your self-esteem.

5
The Wolfman

dolescence also brings a change in the appearance of a guy's face. Not only might his complexion change, but he'll start growing hair where once his skin was smooth and free of any kind of whiskers. Guys usually develop facial hair between the ages of 13 and 15. Some start at 10, others at 17. It is different for every guy. Some guys are blond and fair, so their facial hair is barely noticeable even after it has been growing for a while. Other guys have hair that is coarse and dark and shows right away.

Attitudes about facial hair vary widely, depending on location, the predominant culture, and the norms

of the time. Some cultures view hair as a sign of masculinity, while some think it is unattractive. Since the United States has so many cultures, attitudes about facial hair can vary.

Regardless of the age when it begins, starting to grow facial hair is a rite of passage every guy will go through. The experience is something Brett knows all too well.

Brett's Story

"Next up, batting for the Spartans, number 32, Brett Cooper," the announcer declared.

Regardless of the age when it begins, starting to grow facial hair is a rite of passage that every guy will go through.

The crowd in the stands began to cheer. Some of the kids made wolf howls. Some shouted, "Go,

Wolfman!" Brett held up his bat and tried not to pay attention to them. He hated the nickname almost as much as the reason behind it—all the coarse black hairs that kept springing up across his face.

Brett tuned out the crowd and focused on the ball. He gave the pitcher his best scowl. The pitcher did a windup and then released the ball. Brett swung the bat and missed. He had to tune out the people and those annoying taunts. The pitcher wound

Brett held up his bat and tried not to pay attention to them.

up again. The ball sailed toward Brett. He didn't take his eyes off it. Brett swung his bat a second time. It connected with the ball with a satisfying crack. The ball sailed into right field. As Brett ran past first base and toward second, he heard the kids in the crowd howling. He slid into second base just in time. He'd sent Jason home, and the kids in the stands were going wild.

For what felt like the thousandth time, he wished his dad was in the stands going wild with them. Brett couldn't remember the last time his dad had made it to any of his games. He was always busy working. Whether his games were on a weeknight or a Saturday, his dad could never make it. Brett tried to pretend it didn't matter. Then, he heard a familiar voice shouting his name. He squinted against the lights. Was that really his dad?

Think About It

- How would you have reacted to Brett if you had been in the stands?

- Why did Brett try to pretend it didn't matter that his father wasn't at the game?

- Is it important for kids to have their parents watch them at games or recitals? Why or why not?

Brett's dad was really there. Brett felt so proud and played even harder. When he hit a triple in the third inning, the howls reached a fever pitch. His face flushed hot with shame that his dad was hearing all the teasing.

After the game, Brett's dad took him out for ice cream. As they worked their way through two double-scoop chocolate cones, his dad said, "You handle that bat pretty well."

Brett looked down into his ice cream. "I wish you hadn't heard that," he responded.

"What, all the wolf howls? I'm used to them by now," Brett's dad said.

Brett looked up. "Really? You got those, too?"

Brett's dad scratched his own five-o'clock shadow, which was more like a three-day growth for some men. "It runs in the family, since the beginning of time. Women in our culture used to say being hairy made a man attractive."

Brett snorted, "Girls don't think that about me. They think it's gross."

His dad brought out a box wrapped in silver paper with a gold bow. "That's why I figured you might want this."

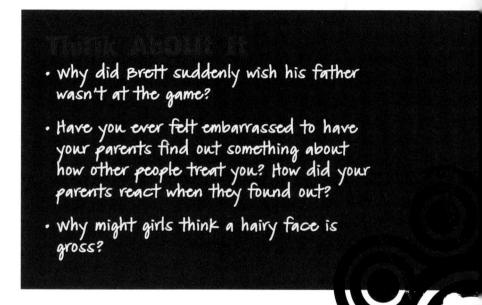

Think About It

- why did Brett suddenly wish his father wasn't at the game?

- Have you ever felt embarrassed to have your parents find out something about how other people treat you? How did your parents react when they found out?

- why might girls think a hairy face is gross?

Brett ripped off the paper and discovered a brand-new electric razor. His dad smiled at him. "My dad gave me his dad's old chrome-plated straight razor. I figured you might want something more state-of-the-art."

"But none of my friends are shaving," said Brett.

"You're getting to be a man now," his dad said. "There's nothing wrong with shaving."

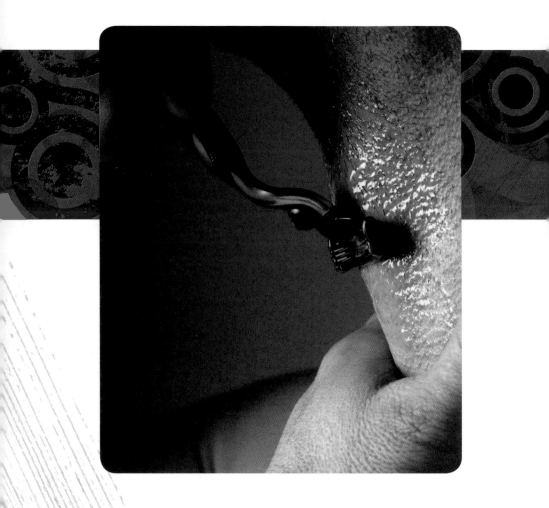

At home that evening, Brett's dad brought out a bottle of pre-shave and showed Brett how to splash it on his face. Next, he showed Brett how to twist his face and puff out his cheeks so the whiskers would stand up for the razor.

"I loved watching you play today," said his dad. "I know I've missed a lot of your season. I'm changing my work hours so I can go to the rest of your games this year."

When Brett was done shaving, he examined himself in the mirror. No more Wolfman. His face was smooth—even handsome—just like it used to be.

Brett's father patted him on the back. "Nice job. You got the hang of it. Anyway, plenty of Hall-of-Famers had nicknames. Wade Boggs was 'Chicken Man.' It just means his fans love him."

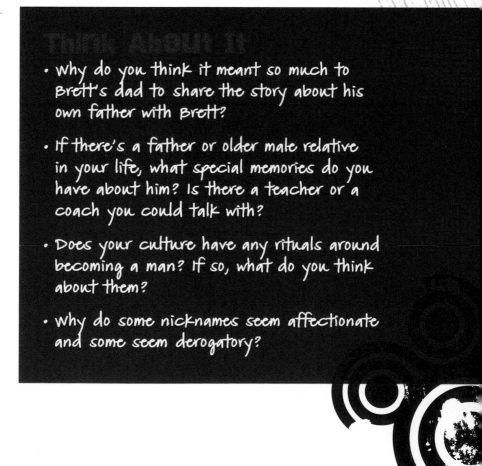

Think About It

- Why do you think it meant so much to Brett's dad to share the story about his own father with Brett?

- If there's a father or older male relative in your life, what special memories do you have about him? Is there a teacher or a coach you could talk with?

- Does your culture have any rituals around becoming a man? If so, what do you think about them?

- Why do some nicknames seem affectionate and some seem derogatory?

With the onset of menstruation, a girl has a definitive marker for when she crossed the boundary out of girlhood. A guy's changes, from shifting body shape to growing body hair, usually take place more gradually. For most guys, there is no one moment they can point to and say, "I'm a man now." A young man is often left to discover for himself how to define his own manhood and what it really means.

It is crucial for guys to have healthy male role models to show the appropriate behaviors of a mature man. Such a mentor could be a father, an uncle, an older brother, or a coach. Usually, a man who has experienced what a guy is going through may connect with him, not just with advice, but in a deep trust. The man has learned from his own experiences, sees what is going on with the guy, and can offer advice. Feeling that your mentor is proud of you and the choices you make is important to most guys growing up.

Work It Out

If you feel embarrassed about having too much facial hair, there's no reason not to start shaving. Ask your father, older brother, or other adult male to show you how to do it. The major choice is between an electric shaver and a blade. Mostly, it comes down to personal choice and trying different options.

Most cultures used to have specific ceremonies or rituals to mark a guy's passage into manhood. Some, such as the Jewish faith, still practice them. A number of organizations, including Outward Bound and Rite of Passage Journeys, are creating new rituals to help mark a guy's growth into manhood—and they can be a lot of fun.

Never share a razor blade with anyone. Blades can carry blood-borne illnesses and spread bacterial or fungal skin infections. If you share a razor, change to a fresh blade. If you share an electric razor, disinfect it with alcohol before each use.

The Last Word from Tad

Learning to shave can be an opportunity to bond with an important male figure. One of my proudest moments with my dad was when he bought me my first razor and showed me how to use it. He told me how his dad taught him to shave. It was hard to believe that my big dad had ever been my age. I still remember the smell of my dad's aftershave. It's a memory I'll always treasure. I hope you have the same experience and someday pass it on to your own son.

6
The Ape Man

hen you start to grow body hair—and how much you grow—is yet another body change that you can't really control. Like facial hair, various cultures have different beliefs about how much body hair is desirable. It's pretty common for men to have "too much" or "too little," according to society—even though the right amount is actually what your body grows naturally.

If you've got a lot of body hair, but the current norm is less hairy (or vice versa), you might feel like you stick out every time you take your shirt off. Steven tried taking extraordinary measures to fit in, with some uncomfortable results.

Steven's Story

"But you love the beach," Steven's mom said as she folded towels and slid them into a bag with sunscreen and a Frisbee.

"I don't wanna go," Steven said from the couch, behind his book.

"We're going, and that's that," proclaimed his dad as he closed the lid on the cooler with a bang.

"Fine," responded Steven, slamming the door on his way out to the car. He didn't say a word on the way to the beach. When they got there, he spread out his towel and immediately opened his book again.

If you've got a lot of body hair, but the current norm is less hairy (or vice versa), you might feel like you stick out every time you take your shirt off.

Steven's little sister, Paige, snatched up his book. "C'mon into the water! You can read anytime."

"Give that back!" He ran after her, shouting, "Mom, tell her to give it back!"

Mom held out her hand. "Paige, book. Steven, please take your sister to the water. I'd appreciate it if you would look after her while I get us situated."

Steven knew it was useless to argue, but he didn't know what else to do. He'd already seen a couple of cute girls from his school on the beach. He couldn't take off his shirt and let them see what a Neanderthal he was. But he'd be an even bigger dork if he was the only one wearing a shirt, so Steven pulled it off.

Paige burst into laughter. "You've got more fur than my teddy bear!"

Think About It

- How do you think you would feel if you were in Steven's position?

- Why didn't Steven want to tell his parents why he didn't want to go to the beach? How do you think they would have reacted?

Steven spent the afternoon in the water. If he kept his body under the waves, no one would see his furry chest. At one point, Erica called to him. He knew Erica from math class and really wanted to go talk to her. Instead, he pretended not to hear her.

That night, Steven was miserable. He couldn't
spend the whole summer avoiding the beach. There
had to be something he could do. He snuck into the
bathroom and tried using his dad's razor on his chest,
but the hair was so thick that it got caught in the
razor and really hurt when he pulled out a bunch of it
by the roots.

Steven went to the Internet for help. He found
a Web site for a laser process that looked pretty good,
but it was really expensive. He was sure he'd need
his parents' permission, too. Since shaving wasn't an
option unless he had a lawn mower, the only thing
left seemed to be waxing—pour melted wax on
yourself, let it dry, then just pull it and the hair off. It
seemed that women did it all the time on their legs,
so he guessed he could handle it.

Think About It

- Why was Steven so desperate to remove the hair from his chest? Have you ever felt that desperate about something?

- Have you done something without consulting someone who might be more knowledgeable? What happened?

- Why do you think some products or procedures need an adult's permission?

Steven ordered a waxing kit. For the next couple of weeks, he made sure he was the first one to search the mailbox every day so that no one else in the family would find out about it. When the kit finally arrived, he waited until everyone was asleep to use its contents. He snuck down to the kitchen and put the wax in the microwave. He took off his shirt. The hot wax burned when he poured it onto his skin.

He remembered how painful the razor had been when it only pulled out a couple of hairs. Now he was going to do his entire chest. Maybe this wasn't such a great idea after all. But the wax had already hardened. It was too late to stop now. He took a firm grip on the wax strip and pulled, fast, just like when you remove a bandage from a cut or scrape.

The pain was unbelievable. He howled in agony. He heard his parents stirring upstairs. He threw on his shirt and crept back to his room. Steven was in such pain that he had trouble sleeping. The next morning, he looked at himself in the mirror. He had a red rash and a bare patch, and it still burned. There was no way he was going to do any more waxing. He didn't know what else to do.

THINK ABOUT IT

- why do you think Steven feels he has to sneak around?

- what could he have done differently that might have been more helpful to him?

- what are some things Steven could do now to help his situation?

Almost everyone feels self-conscious about his or her body at some time or another. Society's "ideal" bodies are everywhere we turn. You can feel a lot of pressure to try to fit in, even if your body is naturally different.

Body hair can be deceptively hard to change. Keeping your chest—or your back—hairless is a much more difficult undertaking than, say, shaving her legs is for a girl. Your body hair is right just the way it is. However, if you do decide you want to get rid of it, it is better to seek professional help. Unsupervised waxing or shaving in awkward places can lead to burns, cuts, rashes, and skin infections.

Work It Out

Body hair—or the lack of it—is just a fashion. A lot of guys look just like you when they take their shirts off. And plenty of people find body hair attractive.

If you do want to remove your body hair, it is safest and easiest to have it done professionally. Talk to your parents about what options are available, and seek a reputable salon.

Look closer at celebrities, athletes, and other people on television and in magazines. You'll find that plenty of men who are widely considered attractive have body hair like yours.

The Last Word from Tad

"It takes courage to grow up and become who you really are." The American poet E. E. Cummings wrote those words, and he was right. You know you should try to be happy with yourself, but it's not always easy. It's tempting to change who you are to fit in. So, every time you don't—every time you wear what you want or follow an interest or make an original decision—pat yourself on the back. It's amazing how good it feels to not care what other people think.

7
The Out-of-Control Face

During adolescence, a guy tries on many roles and explores different interests to build his identity. He may want to join the football team or start a band. He may try different clothes and hairstyles to discover a look that really works for him.

Other forces are changing his looks, too. His hormones may make him taller, expand his chest and larynx, and cause facial and body hair to grow. With so many chemical changes going on, acne may result. All his efforts to build an attractive new image for himself can be disrupted by acne. And having acne can be scary because it's hard to know if it will get better or get worse, or how long

it will stay. Sometimes, acne can leave a guy feeling desperate, just like Ryan.

Ryan's Story

Ryan wailed through the last licks on his guitar, shredding the whammy bar. He brought the neck up and howled

Having acne can be scary because it's hard to know if it will get better or get worse, or how long it will stay.

the final notes of the song just as Jay, the drummer, slammed out the final beat. Ryan tried to slide forward into the splits, but he just whacked his knee on the floor and strained his crotch.

"Man, you're never gonna get that by Friday," said Jay.

Ryan winced in pain. "Sure I will. I just have to keep practicing. I still have a few more days. Don't worry. You'll see."

"You gotta take special classes to do that stuff, like gymnastics or yoga or something. You can't just do the splits!"

Ryan unplugged his guitar and set it on its stand. "Let's eat, I'm starving," Ryan proclaimed as he climbed the basement stairs and threw a package of pizza rolls in the microwave. When the timer dinged, he put some on a plate and handed them to Jay, who just stared at him.

"Dude, you spill some on your face?"

Ryan checked his reflection in the microwave door. Zit city. "Oh, that? Got it under control."

"You better," Jay responded.

After Jay left, Ryan looked in a mirror. His zits were multiplying like an alien invasion force. Friday was so important. Ryan, Jay, and the other members of Black River Wind had been busting their butts to get into the Battle of the Bands. Usually, it was only older kids, but the guy at the audition liked them so much he said he'd make an exception.

Think About It

- Do you think Ryan is as unconcerned about his acne as he says he is? Why does he act that way?

- Why would a guy hide his worries from his friends?

As the front man of his band, Ryan had to look good—no, great. Plus, Haley and Alexis were going to be at the competition, and they said they were bringing their friends. The competition was only four days away. Today's mail had already come, so that made it really only three days left for his miracle cure to arrive and work its magic. In the last month, since he'd started taking his acne seriously, Ryan tried every acne remedy he could get at the drugstore without a prescription. Nothing seemed to work.

Then one day, he found an e-mail in his inbox. He'd almost deleted it with the rest of the spam, but something made him open it. He knew all the promises were probably too good to be true, but the testimonials from the Web sites seemed so real. Even if the before and after pictures really were doctored, it seemed like his last hope. Besides, they promised a money-back guarantee.

Think About It

- Have you ever done something even when you knew better? How did it turn out?

- What is the difference between being afraid to do something and feeling you shouldn't?

- Does a money-back guarantee mean a product is legitimate? Why or why not?

The next day, the package finally came. Ryan plucked it out of the mailbox and hurried to his room. In his haste, he barely read the instructions. You pour it out and put it on. "How hard can that be?" he whispered, as he rubbed the stuff on his face.

"Oooow!" Ryan yelled. It stung like it was burning off his flesh. He hoped that was good—a sign that the product was working to get rid of his acne. But when he looked in the mirror, Ryan saw that his face was bright red, as though he had just scrubbed it with sandpaper. And it was puffy. He looked as though he'd stuffed his cheeks with cotton.

He couldn't go to school looking like this. Ryan stayed in his room all day, hoping the redness would fade and the swelling would go down. He felt so ashamed that he'd ordered the product.

By Friday night, it hadn't gotten much better. He really didn't want to go to the band competition,

but he couldn't let Jay down. He'd just have to go up on stage in front of everybody looking less than great, less than good—well, just plain awful.

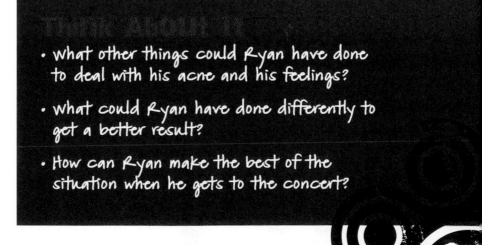

- what other things could Ryan have done to deal with his acne and his feelings?

- what could Ryan have done differently to get a better result?

- How can Ryan make the best of the situation when he gets to the concert?

Acne can be a complicated challenge. Sometimes, it will simply go away on its own over time. More severe cases may cause permanent scarring if left untreated or treated the wrong way. Making the right choice now may have important consequences for the rest of a guy's life. A doctor can prescribe a reliable treatment plan to achieve the best possible results.

Not all medications may be right for all people. A person with more oily skin may benefit from a treatment that dries out the skin. That same treatment, when taken by a person with drier skin, may cause severe irritation or a rash that's worse than the acne.

As much as great sunglasses, a blond streak, or clear skin may help a guy feel good about his image, true relationships are based on identity: a person's attitude about life, his sense of humor, his talents, and his hobbies. Your identity is composed of all the things that are truly you, that no person or circumstance can ever take away. Your identity is much more important than your image, which will change throughout your life. And it's only your identity that you have complete control over— who you are and how you see yourself, not how others see you.

1. If you have severe acne, see a doctor. If left untreated, it can lead to scarring.

2. Acne is caused by hormones. It has to do with your genes, too, and could be related to medication you're taking. But dirt doesn't cause acne. Avoid scrubbing too hard, which irritates the skin further.

3. Another myth is that eating greasy foods causes acne. It's good to stay away from greasy food in general, but not because it causes acne.

4. Many types of alternative therapies follow practices other than traditional medicine, including homeopathic, herbal, or dietary treatments. While many people believe they have achieved good results with such products, others question their effectiveness. Use with caution.

The Last Word from Tad

It's easy to be swayed by advertising that promotes an image or a look you want to have. Be careful when considering a new product. Read the label to determine if something is right for your skin or hair type. Understand your body and what it needs, and you will get through the physical challenges adolescence often presents.

8

The New Body

Change is hard. Thankfully, most changes during adolescence are gradual—and expected. And everybody's going through the same stuff. But what happens when a change isn't typical? What do you do when your whole life turns upside down?

Ramon was a guy who thought he had it all sorted out. But when tragedy struck, he had to find a whole new way to live in the world.

Ramon's Story

Ramon kept his breath and his pace steady, focusing on the finish line. It was another Saturday morning and another cross-country meet for school.

"Go, Ramon, go!" he could hear his dad yell.

"Woo-hoo!" his mom's voice followed.

Ramon picked up the pace and sprinted to the finish line. Like so many of his other meets, Ramon came in first. He stopped and took a water bottle from his coach.

"Good job, Ramon. You tied your best time."

Running was Ramon's life. For as long as he could remember, he just wanted to run. Ramon's mom

But what happens when a change isn't typical? What do you do when your whole life turns upside down?

regularly talked about how he would never stop as a little boy. He just wanted to go, go, go.

After the meet, Ramon and his family went out to eat. It had become their Saturday routine: meet and eat. The rest of the afternoon, Ramon focused on homework and then watching a little TV. That night, he was going out with Brian and Jake. There was a new movie they had been waiting months to see. It had finally come out.

Brian pulled up to Ramon's house at 6:00, right on time. "Bri's here, Mom. Gotta go," Ramon yelled.

"Okay, honey. You may want to take an umbrella. It's supposed to rain tonight, and the sky's looking pretty gloomy," she said.

"We're not really going to be outside. I'll run to the car," Ramon replied. "See ya later."

But that night, things didn't go as planned.

On the ride home from the movie, another car skidded out of control on the wet road and slammed into the car Ramon and his friends were in. One moment, he was laughing about a funny scene in the movie and the next, he was in the hospital surrounded by machines and doctors.

His whole body seemed to be in pain. He could move his arms and scratch his nose, but he couldn't move his right leg. He looked down the length of his body under the covers. His shape was way too narrow below his waist. He panicked. "Where is my leg?" he screamed. A nurse came over and injected something into the tube that ran into Ramon's arm, and he promptly drifted into a deep sleep.

When Ramon awoke, his parents were sitting on one side of him. His mom was stroking his hair.

Her eyes were puffy, and she was trying to hide that she had been crying. His dad stood next to her, holding her hand. "Morning, Ramon. It's good to see you awake. How do you feel?" He looked over to the tall silver-haired man standing at his other side.

"This is Doctor Wilson," Ramon's dad explained. "He's been taking care of you. You were in a car accident. We're just glad you're okay." Ramon looked down his body again, at the gaping emptiness where his leg should be. "Your leg was pinned underneath the car, Ramon. It had to be amputated to get you free. I'm sorry, son."

"Brian and Jake are okay, too. They'll be by to see you later," Ramon's mom explained.

Ramon looked around at the adults. *His mom, his dad, the doctor, how could they be so calm?* he thought. *Didn't they understand what this meant?*

"Now I'm a freak! I wish you had just let me die!" he screamed.

Think About It

- what is the most challenging experience you've had? where did you find resources to get through it?

- Have you ever just wanted everyone to leave you alone? what was that like? why did you feel that way?

- why did Ramon say he'd rather die than live without his leg? Do you think he meant it?

After Ramon got home from the hospital, everyone treated him differently. His cross-country teammates had all signed the big poster that read "Welcome Back, Ramon!" No one talked about the accident. That night, Ramon's mom made his favorite dinner: lasagna and garlic bread. Ramon started feeling a little better. When his little sister tried to steal his pudding, he batted her across the table with one of his crutches, and the whole family laughed. It felt good. They hadn't laughed together since before Ramon's accident.

After dinner, Ramon's mom handed him a brochure showing guys playing basketball in

wheelchairs. "Look how happy they are. I know how much you love sports, honey," she said.

"I don't love sports, Mom," Ramon replied. "I love running. Running! Basketball sucks!" Ramon grabbed his crutches and headed out the front door. It slammed behind him.

Ramon's dad quickly followed and sat on the steps beside him. "We just want to help you," he said as he sat down on the back step beside his son.

Ramon couldn't hold back the tears anymore. "No one can help me, Dad. Just leave me alone."

Think About It

- How would you have treated Ramon when he got back from the hospital?

- Have you ever known someone with a physical disability? Was it awkward to talk to that person? What did you do?

- Why did Ramon get so mad at his dad?

Ramon's dad put his arm around Ramon's shoulder. "Over summer break, there's going to be a camp for boys in similar situations."

Ramon pulled away. "I don't want to be with all the rejects."

Ramon's dad told him to try it for a week. If he didn't like the camp, he could come home. Ramon reluctantly agreed.

Once his injury healed, Ramon got a prosthetic leg. Two weeks later, he went to summer camp. His first night at the camp, Ramon was dropping off his food tray at the dishwasher when another guy with an artificial leg came up behind him. "I'm Marcus." He pointed down at his fake leg. "And this is Super-Marcus."

"I suppose you're one of those wheelchair basketball guys," Ramon replied, rolling his eyes.

"Nah," Marcus smiled. "Hockey."

Ramon turned around. "Hockey? Like ice skates and sticks and stuff?"

"Sure. It's the best," Marcus explained. "You get to go super fast."

Ramon liked fast. "But I couldn't skate that well when I had two legs," he protested.

"So, you can skate better with your super leg," said Marcus.

"No way! . . . Really?" Ramon said, looking down at his fake leg. "How can that be?"

"You just haven't gotten used to it yet," Marcus said. "It's true. C'mon, I'll show you."

Ramon shrugged. "Okay," he said, following Marcus out the door. He had to admit, he was curious. "Sounds cool," he added, smiling.

Ramon shrugged. "Okay," he said, following Marcus out the door. He had to admit, he was curious. "Sounds cool," he added, smiling.

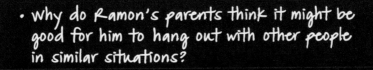

- why do Ramon's parents think it might be good for him to hang out with other people in similar situations?

- why does Ramon call the others rejects? Is he being hard on himself?

Adjusting to major life changes can be a long process. Sometimes, a guy may want it to all happen at once. Other times, it feels to him as though the process will never end. Well-meaning adults will likely want to help him get through it, when all he may want is time to work on his feelings, get used to his new situation, and figure out what it means for his life. It may be especially hard if, like Ramon, he had a dream that no longer seems possible.

A guy may feel deeply angry that his life has taken such a sudden, irrevocable turn. He may not understand his anger, or he may feel bad about it and want it to go away. He may even feel guilty about feeling angry. All these emotions are natural. At first, the anger may feel frightening or overwhelming because of its intensity. Over time, its fierceness diminishes to a more manageable level. Eventually, acceptance takes it place, especially as a guy finds new interests and passions.

Work It Out

1. Even if you can't do what you want to do, there are always plenty of things to enjoy about life. Make a list of all the things you love that you can still do.

Explore new opportunities. Your doctor may have suggestions. Make a list of new things to try, even if you're not sure whether you'll like them or not.

There are times when you may not want to talk, and that's fine. But spending time with others who are going through similar issues can be helpful in many ways. Just finding out that you are not alone can be very helpful.

The Last Word from Tad

It can be easy to think of someone with a disability as being different from you. Ramon's car accident changed him physically, but he was still Ramon. Sometimes, people feel awkward around people with disabilities because they're not sure how to act. Should you open the door for people in wheelchairs, for example? You don't want to insult them by doing things for them that they can easily do themselves. Ask yourself how you would like to be treated if you were in that situation. You'd probably want people to be honest and normal with you. So, if you don't know what to do, ask. "Can I get that door for you?" Presto. Now you know what to do.

9

The Shower Nightmare

For a guy who feels insecure about himself, showering with other guys after gym class can be a scary experience. A guy may feel awkward about his size, or lack of size, or whether or not he has pubic hair yet.

Guys often check out each other for size. Everyone is trying to figure out if they are normal. The locker room is one place where some guys try to establish their dominance by picking on others. They may use bullying and teasing to hide their own insecurities. Raj has had enough of being bullied in the shower after gym class. Today, he has a new plan for dealing with the problem.

Raj's Story

Raj had no one else left to talk to, no more equipment to put away, and no more imaginary trash along the side of the bleachers to pick up. He was playing a dangerous game with the clock. If he timed it just right, Raj would have about ten seconds to wash off the sweat from gym class before throwing on his clothes and scrambling to get to Spanish.

A big group of guys came out the door, and Raj figured it might be safe to head to the shower. Besides, he couldn't wait much longer. He ran to his locker and pulled out his stuff as quickly as he could. He took

A guy may feel awkward about his size, or lack of size, or whether or not he has pubic hair yet.

off his shirt and wrapped his towel around himself before dropping his shorts. He grabbed some soap and hustled to the shower room.

When he got there, Raj's heart sank. It was still filled with guys laughing and snapping each other with their towels. Ignoring them, Raj left his own towel and underwear on the bench and snuck past them to the shower in the far corner. Maybe no one would notice him. He turned the knob and gasped as the hot spray hit his chest. He was half-soaped when he heard Nathan and his friends yelling as they came into the room.

"Hey Raj! Why you hiding over there? Don't want anyone to see Teeny Weenie?" Nathan shouted across the room. The other guys guffawed.

Just wash off the soap and get out of here fast, Raj told himself. He turned away from Nathan and his friends and did his best to hide so no one could see how small he was.

"Is this your underwear? I didn't know it came in extra small," Nathan said as he grabbed Raj's towel and underwear from the bench.

"Hey, give that back!" Raj exclaimed.

"Teeny Weenie speaks!" Nathan replied as he balled up the towel and underwear and threw them to Andrew.

Raj ran at Andrew, almost slipping on the slick floor. Any minute, the bell would ring, making him late for Spanish. But he had to get his stuff back. Andrew tossed it back to Nathan. Raj ran at him. When he was almost there, Nathan chuckled and threw the balled up towel and underwear over Raj's head, back to Andrew.

"Come on! Give it back!" Raj yelled. He had never felt more humiliated in his life.

Nathan laughed. "You heard him, Andy. Give it back!"

"Sure," said Andrew as he threw Raj's towel and underwear into a big pool of dirty water. "Oops! Sooooorry," he said, laughing.

Think About It

- How else might Raj have reacted to Nathan?
- How do you think Raj could have behaved to keep the bullies from picking on him?
- Why do you think Nathan and Andrew picked on Raj? Was there something other than size going on?

Raj grabbed the cold, wet towel and wrapped it around his waist before Nathan could grab it again. He was so ashamed, he just wanted to die.

"Man, you just got punked!" said Andrew. "Punked by the wild men!" Andrew howled and threw down his towel. He sprang up and hung naked from the doorframe, swinging from side to side like an ape.

Raj slunk to his locker with the cold sopping towel, dripping as he went. He tried wringing out his

underwear, but it was still too damp. He'd have to
go without. As Raj slid on his pants over his still-wet
body, he watched Andrew's antics. He was thankful
that Andrew was drawing all the attention now,
hanging from the doorway, letting his naked body
swing. Then Raj realized something. Andrew wasn't
any bigger than he was.

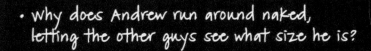

Think About It

- why does Andrew run around naked,
  letting the other guys see what size he is?

- If Andrew is the same size as Raj, why do
  you think no one picks on him?

- what do you think would help Raj feel
  and act more proud of his body?

Just as with everything else during puberty, guys' penises start growing at different times. The size of every part of a guy's body depends on many factors, including genetics and body type. This means that any given locker room will be filled with guys who have a range of sizes. The size of a nonerect (flaccid) penis can be affected by many things. Cold makes muscles contract to bring the penis closer to the body to conserve heat, and different bodies have higher or lower cold tolerance.

Another factor contributing to size is where the penis connects to a guy's body. Some guys' penises are rooted closer to the front of their bodies, thus appearing larger, while some are further back between their legs, thereby appearing smaller.

Some guys worry about their size. It's important to remember that there are many different penis sizes and shapes, and most healthy penises are closer to the same size when they are erect. As your body changes during puberty, your penis size will also change. And, though you may have heard differently, size really doesn't matter.

1. It's usually best to first try to deal with bullying situations yourself by standing tall and being assertive. You can also "buddy up" and make sure that you and your friends look out for each other. If you ever feel in danger, report the situation immediately to someone with the authority to make it stop, such as a parent or teacher.

2. Questions about penis size, shape, or function are some of the worst possible questions to try to find answers to on the Internet, especially since these kinds of queries can invite negative Web sites and chat rooms. As with anything else, be sure you are on a reputable Web site that is sponsored by a medical board, health institute, or other authoritative body. Health classes and libraries are also good resources.

The Last Word from Tad

Looks aren't everything. Attitude and behavior are far more important than appearance. Act as though you are valuable, valued, and important, and others will likely treat you the same way. Self-confidence will bring you more than attention for superficial reasons will bring you. You will be respected.

10
The Fitness Test

It is a teacher's job to help all of his or her students, not just the good ones. As with any subject, a good gym teacher will notice which students are really struggling and design homework to help those students improve their skills. These teachers know that it can be embarrassing for a guy to have less athletic skill than his classmates—especially in gym class. These teachers work hard to make the exercises fun and have a zero-tolerance policy for bullying or name calling.

There are plenty of good gym teachers like that, who really care about their students and put in the time and effort for them. Sometimes, though, gym teachers focus on improving the guys who are already good athletes. They leave the other guys to fend for themselves, to improve on their own, or to feel constantly humiliated. Cody knew this all too well.

Cody's Story

"Co-dy! Co-dy! Co-dy!" All the guys chanted, but Cody could barely focus because of the pain in his arms.

"Let me just make one and I won't argue with mom and dad for a whole week," Cody prayed. He tensed his muscles as hard as he could. The metal pull-up bar seemed so close now, only inches away. He strained every fiber of his body, but his muscles were already shaking under the strain. In desperation, he kicked quickly to buy himself just another quarter inch, but it didn't help.

Cody knew he wasn't supposed to kick. Coach Bell would disqualify you if he caught you doing it too much, but Cody had to risk it. It seemed to bring him just a little closer, but not close enough. He just couldn't get his chin to the bar, no matter how much he wanted it to happen. His muscles felt like he'd been hanging from the bar all day. They burned so much he almost screamed.

Sometimes, though, gym teachers focus on improving the guys who are already good athletes. They leave the other guys to fend for themselves, to improve on their own, or to feel constantly humiliated.

Cody's arms trembled. His fingers hurt. He couldn't hold on anymore. His grip broke, and he fell to the gym floor, exhausted. He wanted to run away and disappear. Coach Bell blew his whistle and then told Cody to return to the sidelines.

Garrett walked calmly up to the bar, chuckling at Cody. "Yeah, Cody. Out of the way. Don't know why we even waste our time on you."

Garrett finished two perfect pull-ups before Cody could even crawl out of the way. "Nice work, Garrett," Coach Bell said, patting him on the back. "I expected nothing less."

Think About It

- Have you ever tried to do something you just couldn't do, no matter what? How did you respond?

- what could Coach Bell have done to help Cody? why do you think he didn't do it?

- what could Cody have done to help himself? why do you think he didn't do it?

The worst part was, this was only the practice test. Cody would have to do it all over again in two weeks—the pain and the humiliation would all be repeated. And Coach Bell would do nothing to help

or encourage Cody. Garrett, however, was the coach's prize athlete and got all the attention and coaching.

After school, Kyle ran up to Cody. "Hey, Cody, I saw you fall off the bar again," he said.

"Yeah, what's it to you?" Cody responded.

"Didn't you see me fall off? Those pull-ups suck, so I decided that today was the last time they're gonna kick my butt. A bunch of us are getting together to practice. We've got two whole weeks! Wanna come?"

Cody was surprised. "You mean spend our own time doing pull-ups without anyone forcing us to?"

"We'll do other stuff, too," Kyle said. "Just think how surprised Garrett's gonna be when he sees us really doing stuff."

Cody thought about Kyle's offer. It would be cool to have some actual muscles and not be afraid of the test when it came. But what if he couldn't do it? What if he spent all that time for nothing?

"Nah," he said. "I've got too much homework."

Kyle trotted off. "You know where to find us if you change your mind."

For the next two weeks, Cody saw Kyle and his friends working hard after school. They'd rotate between all the fitness tests they had to perform in gym class: pull-ups, push-ups, sit-ups, and the run. One afternoon, he heard a shout and looked over to see Kyle with his chin above the bar.

Cody thought about how he'd feel if he showed everyone that he really could do it. But that was just what Coach Bell wanted. He gave them the stupid pretest to fool them all into working hard and spending all their free time doing what he wanted them to. Besides, it was too embarrassing to admit that Kyle had been right all along.

Think About It

- would you join Kyle's group?

- why does Cody decide not to join Kyle and the other guys in preparing for the fitness test? What do you think of his decision?

- why does Cody think it would be embarrassing to admit Kyle was right? Have you ever let embarrassment stop you from something you really wanted?

As the test grew closer, Cody grew more depressed. He knew he should be practicing, but it was just too hard. The two weeks passed. Finally, the day came for the real test.

Kyle could still only do one pull-up, but he flashed everybody on his team the victory sign and they all clapped. Cody was next. He braced himself for the walk to the sand pit, and he found himself in the same situation he'd been in two weeks earlier. Surrounded by his classmates, Cody hung from the bar, straining, as many of the guys shouted his name, "Co-dy! Co-dy! Co-dy!"

Surrounded by his classmates, Cody hung from the bar, straining, as many of the guys shouted his name, "Co-dy! Co-dy! Co-dy!"

Think About It

- Why does doing something with a group of people, such as Kyle training with his friends, make a task seem easier?

- Have you ever been tempted to give up but stuck with something difficult anyway? What was that experience like?

- What else could Cody have done to make a better outcome for himself?

When people talk about peer pressure, they tend to emphasize the bad aspects of it. But a guy can use peer pressure for good things, too. When a group of people work together on a goal that's hard for all of them, the work can feel a lot easier. The friendly pressure encourages each one to work a little harder and give it a little more, even if he'd normally quit if he were by himself. It can also provide encouragement, inspiration, and consolation when the going gets tough. Though the work itself may never be enjoyable, it can help to laugh with friends. Laughter creates endorphins, the body's natural, healthy drugs that actually do make things easier.

Adults use positive peer pressure and group support for many reasons. Some use it to get fit, while others use it to become more successful in business or to overcome their fear of public speaking.

Students at all levels use study groups and sports teams to help each other. If you're having a hard time with something, there may already be a group working together on it. If not, it can be rewarding and empowering to do as Kyle did and create your own.

Work It Out

Getting fit doesn't have to be about forcing yourself to do things you hate. Keep trying different things and you may find something you really enjoy.

Life is full of challenges. If there are situations in your life that you would like to change, write down some ideas about what it would take to change them, and then commit to doing something about them or feeling okay with them as they are.

When you hit a bump in the road, it's your choice whether to feel bad about it or to work hard to do something about it. Taking action proves you are powerful and helps you feel good about yourself.

The Last Word from Ted

Kyle chose to do something about his situation, while Cody chose to do nothing. Cody must accept the responsibility for his choice. If he wasn't going to practice, he wasn't going to improve. Every decision comes with trade-offs and consequences. You don't have to work to change your situation, but then you don't get to complain about it when it doesn't change. When you make an honest choice, you accept that you have full control over the results and are willing to take the consequences of acting or not acting.

A Second Look

All of the guys in this book faced challenges. They felt alone in what they were going through, and many felt jealous of other guys who seemed to be having an easier time. But those other guys were likely confronting rough times of their own. Some of the guys you read about made good choices, and some made choices that weren't the best. But there was always another day to learn from previous choices and make new ones.

Just as taking on demanding tasks in sports or math or drama helps you to do better in those areas, facing challenges in life helps build emotional muscles and shape you into a stronger person. If you didn't work hard and conquer resistance, you'd never grow.

Many guys feel ashamed and embarrassed to talk about the issues faced by the guys in this book and those faced by every guy as he matures. You don't have to face these changes or the challenges of growing up all by yourself. Friends, parents, relatives, teachers, spiritual leaders, counselors—anyone you trust—can be there to get your back. You simply need to reach out. You may be surprised to discover how many of them have been through similar situations.

As you continue to grow and change, remember the lessons learned by the guys in the book and the people you know and talk to. Remember, too, that the best lives are a good balance of work and play. Try to find humor even in the most challenging situations. Good luck, don't stress too much, and have fun!

Good luck,

Tad

Remember, a healthful life is about balance. Now that you know how to walk that path, pay it forward to a friend or even yourself! Remember the Work It Out tips throughout this book, and then take these steps to get healthy and get going.

- Take charge of your life. If there's something you feel bad about and want to change, find a way to change it. Make a plan, get the resources and help you need, and take action. Even if you can't change physical aspects of yourself, you can change how you and others think about them.

- Spending a lot of time on the sidelines of your life wishing things were different doesn't help you get what you want. You can experience your feelings and stay in the game at the same time. Find the good things in your life or create them, and keep taking steps to reach your goals.

- Other people treat you the way you treat yourself. A little attitude goes a long way. Even if you don't always feel good about yourself, treat yourself well and try to have a sense of humor about what's going on. Others will appreciate your confidence.

- Reach out to others. Getting help or advice from others can make life a lot easier.

- "Think outside the box" may be a cliché, but it's good to remember. It can be easy to get stuck in thinking there are only the obvious answers to questions or issues you may have. Brainstorming and talking to others to get a different perspective can pay off.

- Don't wait for a perfect solution. Weigh the pros and cons, and make sure that you can live with the downsides of whatever you choose.

- Don't give up.

- Don't take things—or yourself—too seriously. You can't control when challenges will happen, but you can control how you react to them. Humor diffuses tension and makes it easier for other people to connect with you. It also releases endorphins that help your body feel better and deal with stress.

Additional Resources

Selected Bibliography

Bell, Ruth, and members of the Teen Book Project. *Changing Bodies, Changing Lives.* 3rd ed. New York: Random House, 1998.

Biddulph, Steve. *Raising Boys: Why Boys Are Different—and How to Help Them Become Happy and Well-Balanced Men.* Berkeley, CA: Ten Speed, 2008.

Meeker, Meg. *Boys Should Be Boys: 7 Secrets to Raising Healthy Sons.* New York: Random House, 2008.

Taguchi, Yosh. *Private Parts: A Doctor's Guide to the Male Anatomy.* New York: Doubleday, 1988.

Further Reading

American Medical Association and Kate Gruenwald Pfeifer. *American Medical Association Boy's Guide to Becoming a Teen.* San Francisco, CA: Wiley, 2006.

Dunham, Kelli. *The Boy's Body Book: Everything You Need to Know for Growing Up YOU.* Kennebunkport, ME: Cider Mill, 2007.

Hawkins, Frank C., and Greta L. B. Laube *The Boy's Body Guide: A Health and Hygiene Book.* 2nd ed. Potomac Falls, VA: Boy's Guide Books, 2009.

maranGraphics Development Group. *Maran Illustrated Weight Training.* Boston, MA: Thomson Course Technology PTR, 2005.

Maras, Lynda, and Area Maras. *My Body, My Self for Boys.* 3rd ed. New York: Newmarket, 2007.

Web Sites

To learn more about body issues and physical changes, visit ABDO Publishing Company online at **www.abdopublishing.com**. Web sites about body issues and physical changes are featured on our Book Links page. These links are routinely monitored and updated to provide the most current information available.

For More Information

For more information on this subject, contact or visit the following organizations:

Big Brothers Big Sisters
230 North Thirteenth Street, Philadelphia, PA 19107
215-567-7000
www.bbbs.org
This nonprofit organization provides free-of-charge mentors for youth across the United States. Mentors can help to work out issues as well as provide friendship.

Outward Bound
247 West Thirty-fifth Street, Eighth Floor
New York, NY 10001
212-239-4455
www.outwardbound.org
This nonprofit organization helps youth discover their potential through challenging wilderness experiences.

Glossary

assertive

In a bold or confident way.

dismissive

Showing that something is not important.

endorphins

Naturally occurring hormones in the brain that reduce pain in the body and cause feelings of happiness.

endurance

The ability to continue performing a task for a period of time.

flaccid

Limp, not erect.

hormone

A chemical that affects the function of certain tissues or organs.

irrevocable

Something that cannot be changed.

larynx

An organ in the throat that contains vocal cords, which make sounds when air passes over them; also known as the voice box.

masculinity

Manhood.

mentor

A trusted advisor who can help a young person realize his or her own unique gifts.

prosthetic

An artificial device that takes the place of a part of the body that is missing or damaged.

puberty

The stage of life when a child's hormones begin the process of transforming him or her into an adult.

submissive

Showing obedience without resistance.

Index

About the Author

Tad Kershner's writing has appeared in several magazines, and he has won awards for screenwriting and short fiction. He was a youth-group leader for several years. He lives in the Pacific Northwest with his wife and teenage son, and he enjoys going on adventures with his family and friends, including kayaking, hiking, and biking.

Photo Credits

Shutterstock Images, cover, 3; Mikael Damkier/ iStockphoto, 11; Andrey Popov/iStockphoto, 13; John Rodriguez/iStockphoto, 15; iStockphoto, 16, 21, 36, 71, 75, 95, 96; Pali Rao/iStockphoto, 22, 67; Ju-Lee/ iStockphoto, 24; John Hawthorne/iStockphoto, 26; Wade Ledema/iStockphoto, 31; Andrea Gingerich/ iStockphoto, 32; Linda Bucklin/iStockphoto, 41; Drazen Vukelic/iStockphoto, 42; Dan Brandenburg/iStockphoto, 45; Phillip Holland/iStockphoto, 49; David Meharey/ iStockphoto, 50; Mehmet Dilsiz/iStockphoto, 52; Eric Hood/iStockphoto, 54; Joselito Briones/iStockphoto, 59; Filipe Varela/iStockphoto, 62; Yong Hian Lim/ iStockphoto, 69; Sandra Nicol/iStockphoto, 77; Eva Serrabassa/iStockphoto, 79; James Pauls/iStockphoto, 85; Daniel Mirer/iStockphoto, 86; Bob Ingelhart/ iStockphoto, 89; Feng Yu/iStockphoto, 98;